THE LIPIZZANS
AND THE SPANISH RIDING SCHOOL
Myth and Truth

Elisabeth Gürtler (Ed.)
Barbara Sternthal

THE LIPIZZANS
AND THE SPANISH RIDING SCHOOL
Myth and Truth

Translated by Neil Radford

CHRISTIAN BRANDSTÄTTER VERLAG
VIENNA

TABLE OF CONTENTS

Preface 6

THE BEGINNINGS 8
Happiness is riding horseback 10 · Luxury creatures
for the Habsburgs – a little history 12 · A noble European
lineage on four legs 18

FROM HORSE EXERCISE AREA TO WINTER RIDING SCHOOL 22
The riding school with top-level involvement 24 · Leopold I
and the incomplete riding school 25 ·
A congenial team 27 · The Winter Riding School 30

TIMES AND CONVENTIONS 36
Aristocratic revelry 38 · From the Vienna Congress to the
end of the century 41 · End and new beginning – 1919–1945 43

LIPIZZAN STUD PIBER 50
Imperial idyll 52 · Place of birth 53 · Kindergarten 58 ·
Residency for the seniors 64

THE FINE ART OF RIDING 66
The rediscovered antiquity 68 · Practise, practise, practise! 71 ·
The gaits of the High School 75 ·
Airs on the ground 76 · Airs above ground 78

NO TIME FOR IDLENESS 82
Daily work routine: between stables and tack room 84 · Early risers 88 ·
From Eleve to Senior Rider 93 · Deerskin and combed yarn 95 ·
Holiday time 97

STARS ON THE STAGE 100
Elegance and Harmony 102 · From the young stallions
to the Schoolquadrille 103

APPENDIX 108
Bibliography und Acknowledgement 110 ·
Picture credits 111 · Editorial Team 112

PREFACE

The Spanish Riding School is special in every regard. Just the name alone is enough to arouse interest and conjure up questions. How is it that a world famous institution in the former imperial city of Vienna has »Spanish« in its name followed by »Court Riding School«? As the oldest preserved riding institute in the world, it is still passing on by word of mouth the teachings of the classical equitation of the Renaissance tradition of the *haute école* and has experienced a very long and diversified history.

The name »Spanish« refers to the horses on show here. Their great-great ancestors originate from Spain – from where they were brought to the Austrian Emperor's court during the 16th century. It was not until the end of the 19th century that the name familiar today, »Lipizzans«, became common. These elegant, intelligent horses (also regarded as the oldest breed of cultural horse in Europe) have been appearing at the baroque Winter Riding School for more than 430 years.

Austria has been a republic for hundred years or so. Before then was the rule of the Habsburgs. For centuries, the *haute école* and the mastery of the noble stallions was reserved only for the aristocracy (hence the name »Court« Riding School). This long history and the tradition of horse breeding and riding instruction practised over hundreds of years make the Spanish Riding School quite unique in the world – even now in the 21st century.

The perfected fusion of horse and rider is inimitable and inspires horse lovers from all corners of the globe. But even people who themselves do not ride and who can not comprehend the staggering level of skill and training of horse and human over years keep being fascinated by the overall mastery on view here.

We would now like to invite you to experience and discover this special institution, its history, its magnificent horses, trainers and senior trainers, and also its continued development in a modern, changed world.

Yours,
Elisabeth Gürtler
General Manager of the
Spanish Riding School–Lipizzan Stud Piber

»Living tradition« is the commitment from Elisabeth Gürtler. In the former national championship runner-up in dressage, the team at the Spanish Riding School has a knowledgeable and understanding leader at the head of the company.

THE BEGINNINGS

Above:
The imperial riding
school. Archduke Karl
(later Emperor Karl VI)
on a dapple-grey horse in
the piaffe; on the left,
a chestnut-brown stallion
practises the capriole
under the rider between
the posts, on the right,
an Isabelle-coloured
stallion and a tiger.
Painting by Johann
Georg Hamilton, 1702.

Opposite page:
A dappled horse from the
royal Lichtenstein stud
farm in Eisgrub (Lednice).
Painting by Johann Georg
Hamilton (landscape by
Anton Faistenberger),
1707.

Happiness is riding horseback

For anyone seeing the consummate harmony and elegance with which horses and trainers at the Spanish Riding School perform before their audiences, it is easy to imagine that the bond between man and horse must extend well back in time. We are indeed talking about a period reaching back to about 3000 B. C., perhaps even to 5000 B. C., although archaeologists are not entirely agreed on this. What we are agreed upon, and what appears to be completely logical, is that the integration of the quick, fleet-footed horse (as compared to cattle which were used for both pulling and riding) brought with it many benefits to communities, and in particular has fundamentally changed the lives of peoples in vast expansive grass plains – first and foremost the steppes of Central Asia. The provision of food became more reliable (hunting), long distances could be overcome easier and, above all, more quickly (between watering holes for example) and those on horseback certainly had the upper hand over neighbours who were not.

Depiction of two riders on the Parthenon in Athens.

However, it took some while before our forefathers in the great prehistoric civilizations took to the horse. A puzzle still

confronting those studying the antiquity. The horse was domesticated in the third millennium B. C. and was, from the second millennium onwards, a familiar sight across the whole of Europe. But there are no depictions of riders until the first mellinium. Up to that time, it was highly probable that only lightly harnessed horse teams befitting the rank of king and nobility were used. Horses were already being trained earlier for this purpose. Familiar from the Mesopotamian empire of the Hurriter is the hippological scripture of the Kikkuli (15th century B. C.) which writes not only of the breed, but also of precise feeding, care and running instructions over a period of 184 days (including gaits and distances) to train the horse perfectly for working with carriages.

Xenophon (left) in debate with Socrates. Fresco, Stanze di Raffaello, Vatican.

The 8th century B. C. saw larger horses being bred and the merits of cavalrymen over carriage drivers. Now riding was integrated and even became part of the ancient Olympic Games, the second day of which traditionally belonged to horse racing and chariot racing.

Historian, military leader and student of Socrates, Xenophon, whose works *Peri hippikes (On horsemanship)* and *Hipparchikos (The Cavalry Commander)* remained valid into the Renaissance and far beyond, allows us the jump from Greek antiquity to the Renaissance. Both works are notably modern works on the training of the horse and of the rider.

Fundamental here is the partnership between man and animal, not power of one over the other – according to Xenophon, the only way to be able to fully rely on the horse in perilous situations. Xenophon was strictly opposed to violence towards the horse. His principles have survived the centuries and were mainly reinstated in the Renaissance by the masters of horsemanship.

»And it is so that a horse which carries itself so proudly is something so beautiful and worthy of admiration and wonder that all spectators' eyes turn towards it. Nobody gets tired of looking at it as long as it exhibits it magnificence.« *Xenophon*

The moment a person mounted a horse, it became a status symbol for nobility and monarchs. And not only that – riding has considerably impacted the course of history. Without its *Equites*, rich citizens who were able to afford their own horses and armament to go with them and who assumed a special position within the army, the Roman empire would never have achieved its immense expansion; Dschingis Khan would not have united the Mongolians and conquered vast parts of

Central Asia; Salah ad-Din would not have been so victorious against the crusader lands and the crusaders themselves would not have arrived at the Italian ports from where they set out to conquer the Holy Land. No sooner was man on horseback than it was off to war together. In every culture, in every land.

Fortunately history is not only about war. Riding was always an aristocratic pleasure, something which the High School of horsemanship is still bearing witness to. And of course trade. There would have been no negotiating of trade routes, such as over the Alps from Salzburg to Venice and from Ghent to Lombardy to exchange salt, metals and finely woven fabrics for valuable spices and raw materials from the Orient. Even if goods were loaded in oxen-pulled wagons or carried by donkeys, the accompanying delegates from the large trading establishments in the North were all on horseback.

History is full of legendary horses. Alexander the Great rode on Bukephalos (above) to India. Calligula, Roman Emperor and not prudish in living out his extravagant neurosis, not only gave his horse Incitatus extremely valuable gifts and allowed it to live in its own palace appointed with grand furniture and with its own staff, he also wanted to appoint him consul and give him a seat in the senate.

LUXURY CREATURES FOR THE HABSBURGS
A LITTLE HISTORY

Up to the Late Middle Ages, the riding horse had finally become a proud status symbol of nobility and the monarch, and the rider had become a knight. However, the image of the lovesick nobleman on his proud steed courting his angelic damsel is only consistent with reality in homoeopathic doses. It is more the Cataphracts who present us with reality – heavily armoured riders and horses as a tower of strength of impact warfare.

Their primary intention was to protect the empires north of the Pyrenees and Alps from the dangers in the South and East – from the Moors in Spain with their lightning quick and perfectly trained Arabian horses, and the skilled bowmen of the Turks who gave the impression that riders were conjoined with the backs of the horses.

Horses in Northern and Eastern Europe were strong and heavy with coarse bones, those of the »enemies of the Christian west« were very different – sensitive, lively and yet gentle, elegant, agile and quicker than the wind. On the fringe of Europe, in Al-Andalus, the Moors empire between Sevilla, Córdoba and Granada, in this flourishing ancient civilisation incomprehensible and reprehensible to Catholic Europe, these thoroughbred Arabian horses belonged just as much to the aristocratic self-image as palace gardens, poetic arts and lute music.

But the Moors not only brought with them Arabian horses, they also brought wild Berber horses, originating from the North African Atlas mountains and said to have the heart of a lion. And in Spain they came across an Iberian horse breed which had been extremely popular with the Romans and which had been spoken highly of by Plinius the Older and Virgil. These three breeds, Arabian, Berber and Iberian, formed the genetic basis for a new, unusually beautiful, intelligent and docile breed of horse whose breeding began under the Kalifs of Al-Andalus and which ultimately, as with the thoroughbred Arabian horse, was used for the refinement of virtually all European horse breeds long after the end of the reign of the Moors in Southern Spain.

> The Moors had brought their mounts with them from the Orient and kept in part to the purity law passed down in the Koran. This is because, according to legend, these fascinating animals were direct descendents of Mohammed's obedient five mares Abayyah, Saqlawiyah, Kuhaylah, Hamdaniyah and Hadbah and it was Mohammed himself who introduced the decree enabling the breeding of one's own horses *asil* (purely). It is the Arabian horse which to this day is still regarded as the oldest domestic animal line in the world.

The Renaissance period, understood to be a reincarnation of the antiquity, saw the revitalisation of horsemanship and horse breeding onto a new plain. The *divertissements* of the aristocracy became more exquisite, villas in the countryside were accessible and noble, agile horses were required. The gentry did not ride to simply get from A to B or to defeat enemies, it was simply for pleasure. No longer required for this were heavy war horses but agile hunting and elegant carriage horses.

Rediscovering the classic antiquity also meant that Xenophon's ancient teachings on horsemanship were moved from the back shelves of libraries to reading desks, and taken for example by Neapolitan Federigo Griso in his textbook on horses and riding. Every self-respecting European court had its stud farms where expensive horses were afforded the best possible treatment. For the Gonzaga in Mantua, the Aragonians in Spain and Naples and of course the Habsburgs, horse breeding and the perfected art of riding were not only etiquette, they had

Arabian, Berber and Iberian horse breeds – bred by the Moors from these three lines was the Andalusian, a powerful, frugal, readily teachable new breed of horse, whereby the Iberian horse breed probably had dominance in breeding. When Southern Italy finally fell to the royal dynasty of Spain in the 15th century, horses were exchanged between the two peninsulas. This resulted in another horse breed, the Neapolitaner. It was more difficult, wilder and ineducable compared to the Andalusian, but in terms of appearance it was exactly what the European aristocracy imagined a representable horse should be at this time. Andalusian and Neapolitaner became ancestors of the best European horse breeds – and hence also the Lipizzans.

become a beloved part of their elitist existence.

Habsburg Karl V ruled his empire from Spain, and the so-called Spanish horses – Andalusian and Neapolitan – joined his triumphal procession through Europe. The first of the three early Habsburg horse breeders was Maria of Hungary, a sister of Karl V, who had a Neapolitan stud farm built in Halbthurn. She bequeathed her valuable herd to her nephew, who later became Emperor Maximilian II, son-in-law of Karl V, who also brought back horses from Spain. 1565 saw the passionate horse lover erect for her a horse exercise area in the direct vicinity of his residence, but this was not covered and was hence unusable in poor weather.

The royal Bohemian court stud farm in Kladrub on the Elbe. The stud farm building can be seen in the background. Painting by Johann Georg von Hamilton, around 1756.

The »Kladrub game reserve«, an age-old stud farm given
to him on the occasion of his crowning to King of Bohemia,
became Maximilian's breeding centre. He brought his valuable
horses to Kladrub, which Maximilian's son Emperor Rudolf II
had elevated to the imperial court stud farm in 1579, to start a
breed. The »Spanish« horses from Kladrub were not only intended
to serve as spirited hunting horses, but also mainly as carriage
horses for the modern, elegant carriages now being manufactured
in Kocs in Hungary.

Also dedicated to the breeding of »Spanish« horses was
Emperor Maximilian's youngest brother, archduke Karl II of
Inner Austria, a passionate hunter but also, very much in the
style of a Renaissance ruler, patron of science and the arts, who
ultimately founded the largest Habsburg stud farm in the Trieste
karst. The summer residence of the bishop of Trieste in Lipica,
virtually destroyed after the retreat of the Turks, stood empty.
Karl bought it in 1578
to breed, from 1580,
noble hunting and
cavalry horses from
Andalusians, Neapoli-
tans, powerful Karsts,
thoroughbred Arabians
and other races
cherished by European
courts.

The Karst court stud farm
in Lipica. Painting from
around 1770.

Left:
Philosoph, a white horse from the Lipica stud farm in Karst. Painting by Richard Hamilton, around 1725.

Below:
Cerbero, a Neapolitaner dappled horse, in the capriole. Painting by Johann Georg von Hamilton, around 1721.

Right:
The horse Excellente.
Painting by Johann Georg
von Hamilton, 1720.

Below:
A white Karst horse being
led by an imperial groom.
The horse has magnificent
saddling. Painting by
Johann Georg von
Hamilton (white horse,
around 1740) and Johann
Christian Brand (land-
scape, around 1760).

A NOBLE EUROPEAN LINEAGE ON FOUR LEGS

Establishing Lipica was somewhat difficult. Here, on the sparse rocky ground in the middle of the karst, the paddocks represented dangerous terrain for the tendons and joints of the precious animals. And there was barely any fertile land to establish grazing and oat-growing areas. Another problem was a lack of water – which is why every drop of rain to fall was caught in cisterns.

The start of horse breeding itself was must simpler. This was because both archduke Karl II, the »founder« of Lipica, and his nephew Emperor Rudolf II had a soft spot for horses. And because Rudolf II had a capable ambassador in Spain in Hans Christoph Khevenhüller, nothing stood in the way of importing the noble »Spanish horses«. According to the records in Lipica, 1581 saw six stud stallions and twenty four mares arrive at the newly established Karst stud farm.

Horsebreeding in Lipica ultimately became a matter of personal interest from 1619 when archduke Karl's son become Emperor of the Holy Roman Empire as Ferdinand II . With the incorporation of Inner Austria into the countries of the Habsburg main line, Lipica was also placed under the direct control of the Emperor's head stable master. Following a stud farm instruction from Ferdinand's grandson Emperor Leopold I, Lipica ultimately became an institution of the court.

> But it was a long time before the horses from Lipica were called Lipizzans. This name did not appear until about two hundred years later with Italian spelling (»Lippizans«) which, thanks to a spelling mistake, became the »Lipizzan« familiar today. In the 16th century, the horses were simply called »Spanish« and their milky-white coat was a breeding trend not purposefully pursued until the 18th century.

The stud farm underwent a series of expansions during the course of the following century. New stable and living quarters were built and more and more pasturelands were established despite the sparse natural environment. It was during the reign of Emperor Karl VI (1711–1740) in particular that Lipica underwent considerable expansion by, for example, leasing the large holdings of the Auersperg near Postojna and acquiring assets near Poček, Bile and Pestranek.

The fate of Lipica, where the horses long officially called the »original Spanish from the Karst stud farm« were bred, was changeable. From the evacuation of Napoleon's troops to the consideration of completely abandoning the court stud farm,

Lipica was under threat more than once of becoming a chapter in the history books. But during these years, the stallions which established the stallion lines of today's stars at the Court Riding School were born.

The list of these Lipizzan ancestors reads like a hippophile idea of complete European solidarity – or better still: every name in itself is a noble lineage with selected noble affinity.

Mare herds at the imperial Lipica court stud farm. Painting by Johann Georg von Hamilton, around 1727. Most of the mares in Piber also descend from the families of these six stallions. The brand denotes the particular stallion from which they originate. There are also eighteen mare lines, each formed from an ancestress: Sardinia and Spadiglia from the Karst breed; Stornella and Famosa originate from the Koptschan stud farm in Slovakia; Afrika, Almerina, Englanderia, Presciana, Europa and Rava originally came from Kladrub, Deflorata from Denmark; Gidrana, Djebrin and Mercurio are descended from Arabian mare families, Elien, Miss Wood and Hamad Flora from Vukovar, Croatia, and finally Theodorosta from Bukovina.

Pluto

He was born in 1765 in the royal Danish court stud farm of Frederiksbørg and was a powerful white horse of Spanish ancestry. The stud farm in Frederiksbørg was founded in 1562 by Danish king Frederik II who wanted to breed a horse for classic cavalry from domestic mares as well as Andalusian and Neapolitaner stallions. Breeding itself was induced with some laisser-faire in that the half-wild mare herds in the large paddock were visited every year in spring by selected stallions. Despite this unorthodox breeding method, it produced excellent horses which were highly desired by other European courts. For example, Caterina de' Medici in her Blois castle in the Loire and Philipp II in Madrid were proud owners of majestic Frederiksbørg horses.

Left: Pluto Aquileja

Conversano

The original black horse was born in 1767 and was an original Neapolitaner. This thoroughbred was, nomen est omen, bred in Naples and, by virtue of its noble appearance, was highly desired by worldly and ecclesiastical rulers as a puller of state coaches. The then kingdom of Naples was ruled by members of the Spanish House of Aragon and hence belonged to Spain from the early 16th century. This meant the exchange of horses, in particular Andalusian and the Portugese Lusitanos, was relatively smooth. Crossbreeding was performed between the imported Iberian breeds and those domestic horses whose history could be traced back to the time of the Etruscans.

Right: Conversano Dagmar

Favory

The dun horse was born in 1779 and came from the imperial Kladrub court stud farm in Bohemia, so from the court's own breed. This stud farm was first mentioned in official documents in the 12th century and came under the ownership of Wilhelm von Pernstejn in the 15th century. He was primarily responsible for the expansion, had stud farm buildings constructed and had the river bed of the Elbe changed to benefit pastureland. Crossing with the Spanish and Italian horses which Emperor Maximilian II had brought with him produced a noble breed which was extremely friendly towards people and which was later bred specifically as a carriage horse. White and black horses for jovial and sad occassions at the Habsburg court.

Left: Favory Superba

Neapolitano

The majestic bay horse with the shiny coat was born in 1790. He was born in Polesina in Northern Italy, the area around Rovigo, but was, as Conversano, a purebred Neapolitaner. The area around Neaples was famous for its first-class horses long before the reign of the House of Aragon. They originally came from the Etruscan stud farms in the town of Capua, and apparently even Hannibal himself was an admirer of these noble horses. Crossing with Berbers introduced from North Africa by the Romans and, after the demise of the Roman empire, with Turkish breeds from Byzanz, produced a breed of horse so valuable that King Karl I outlawed its crossbreeding with any other breeds from that point on. An edict which was lifted three hundred years later by the Spaniards in favour of crossbreeding with Spanish horses.

Right: Neapolitano Pastime

Siglavy

Of the Lipica stallions, he was the exotic one with a past. Born in 1810 in Syria, he went to France from where Prince Karl Philipp von Schwarzenberg brought him back. Prince Karl Philipp was first the Habsburg's ambassador to the court of Napoleon and later commander-in-chief of the combined forces fighting against the Emperor of the French. In 1826, Siglavy, the thoroughbred Arabian stallion, the »drinker of the winds«, was acquired for the court stud farm in Lipica where he became an ancestor of a separate Lipizzan line.

Left: Siglavy Materia

Maestoso

The last of the ancestors was a white horse born in 1819 at the Mezhegyes stud farm in Hungary whose father was an original Neapolitaner and whose mother was a hot-blooded Spaniard. The stud farm still exists and can be traced back to its founding by Emperor Josef II who was seeking to put an end to the latent horse shortage within his army. Cavalry captain Csekonics became head of the stud farm, an enterprising follower of his Emperor who was at times lord and master over up to 4000 horses, 10,000 oxen, distilleries and even a sugar factory – spread over an area of 7000 square kilometres.

Right: Maestoso Virtuosa

From Horse Exercise Area to Winter Riding School

Above:
Josefsplatz, probable
location of the horse
exercise area of Emperor
Maximilian II. Engraving
by Salomon Kleiner,
around 1730.

Opposite page:
»Michaels Platz in front of
the royal and imperial riding school«. Drawn and
engraved by Karl Schütz,
1784.

23

The riding school
with top-level involvement

What was once merely a stable for nags, or horses, was converted primarily in the baroque period into a princely stable – magnificently designed steel structures, usually with adjoining riding hall, whose operation was managed, or at least represented, by a high-level aristocratic court official. Supplied by the stud farms in the country, the royal stables in the seats of power became resplendent centres of princely pleasure, but mainly of representation.

The seat of royal power in Vienna also saw the surrendering to this desire to build, the more so as the old Hofburg threatened to become too confining. When the son of Emperor Ferdinand I, Maximilian, the successor to the throne, returned to Vienna after spending several years in Spain, he not only brought with him a

The inner courtyard of the Stallburg – magnificently renovated and with outer stalls for particularly inquisitive stallions.

young wife, initial government experience and a certain generous cosmopolitanism, he also brought a spectacular menagerie, including giant elephants, camels, parrots and noble Spanish steeds. To be able to accommodate the giant royal household of the archduke and his exotic menagerie (befitting his rank), the Emperor ordered the extension of the Hofburg. The result was the Stallburg, a magnificent renaissance building within the complex of the Hofburg, the ground floor of which integrated stables built to Spanish plans. This continues to house the Lipizzans. And in front of the Stallburg, probably where Josefsplatz is today, Maximilian had a horse exercise area (»Ross-Tumblplatz«) built. When this turned out to be none too pleasant (it was not covered and so was exposed to the elements), he had a »Spanish Riding Hall« built for his valuable Iberian freight in 1572. This simple wooden building is the first mention by name of the Spanish Riding School.

> Maximilian trusted only the Spanish in matters concerning his horses. It was Spaniards who bought horses in Naples for the Viennese court and he had also brought back a head stable master, also a Spaniard. Don Francisco Lasso di Castilia served from 1550 to 1570.

The Stallburg could never establish itself as residential quarters or governments building for the Habsburgs. The beautiful Renaissance arcades surrounding the inner courtyard were soon bricked up to protect the imperial art collection. It was not converted back to its original open state until after 1945.

LEOPOLD I
AND THE INCOMPLETE RIDING SCHOOL

The next Habsburg with an eagerness to build was the art-minded Emperor Leopold I who reigned from 1658 to 1705. He was not without controversy but, apart from a series of questionable domestic decisions, he was a very interesting monarch, both literarally and scientifically, who had a gift for languages and who showed great passion, especially for music. During his time in office, Vienna began to develop into a baroque-styled seat of power and was soon to become a cultural centre of Eastern Central Europe.

The Emperor's desire to build was initially concentrated on a fitting new residence and residential building near the Hofburg. The »Leopoldinische Trakt«, as it is still known today, was so advanced on paper in 1660 that Lodovico Burnacini and Filiberto Lucchesi, the Emperor's master builders, were able to commence building work. This took six years, but luck was not on the side of the residents as only two years later the palace burned down, leaving only its foundation walls. Leopold only just managed to escape the blaze with his family, blamed the arson attack on Jews, drove them from the city and ordered the immediate reconstruction (completed in 1681).

Now back safe and secure in their home, the imperial family was able to dedicate itself again to aristocratic representation. And Leopold did this by recalled the wooden »Spanish Riding Hall« which his great great uncle Maximilian II had built in front of the Stallburg. Here, a new riding school was to be built on the exercise area in line with contemporary baroque taste. It was to be a three-storey building – a library in the upper rooms and underneath, on the ground floor, a winter riding school. But Leopold I was mistaken in one regard. He was of

Gundakar, Prince Dietrichstein in a costume for the horse ballet to honour the arrival of the bride of Leopold I. Painting by Jan Thomas, 1667.

the opinion that the danger coming from the Turks was broadly averted, or Vienna was at least immune from Turkish invasion thanks to new city walls – a fatal misjudgement as it turned out in 1683 when Vienna suffered the second siege by the Turks. At any rate, the semi-finished »new riding school« became a victim of the far-reaching cannons of the Ottoman besiegers.

Italian courts had set an example – horse ballets and horse carousels in which horses were ridden, with musical accompaniment, in line with the rules of the High School and in time with the music. To celebrate his wedding to his first wife, Infanta Margareta Teresa of Spain, Leopold I performed the non plus ultra of such a horse ballet. The magnificent celebrations took place in January 1667 in the inner castle yard and one of the main stars was the Emperor in person. Copper engraving by J. Ossenbeeck from work by Nicolaus van Hay, 1674.

Emperor Joseph I (at the very front on white horse) on the Parforce hunt. Painting by Johann Georg von Hamilton, around 1710.

A CONGENIAL TEAM

Joseph I, who succeeded his father Leopold I as Emperor, was a spirited rider who affectionately tamed his horses himself – to the horror of the court. But the realisation of the old Habsburg plan of a representative riding school was left to Josef's successor, his younger brother Karl VI.

Karl VI was an archetypal baroque builder who, to be able

to indulge in building to the quality worthy of an Emperor, gained the services of three brilliant architects, amongst others, to the court – Johann Bernhard Fischer von Erlach, his son Joseph Emanuel Fischer von Erlach and Johann Lucas von Hildebrandt.

Above:
The royal and imperial court stables (now the Museumsquartier).

Opposite page:
The Winter Riding School building. To the right, the »Hoftheater nächst der Burg« which made room for the Michaelertor in 1888.

Coloured copper engravings from works by Tranquillo Mollo, 1825.

This unbeatable triumvirate of first-class builders more or less created the entire baroque face of the possessions of the then Austrian high nobility. It was mainly father and son Fischer von Erlach who created magnificent monuments for the Emperor, and hence for themselves, in Vienna.

Karl VI had a virtually insatiable appetite when it came to the construction of ostentacious buildings to honour the Emperor. At more or less the same time, under his aegis, building work started on Schönbrunn palace, the Favorita summer palace, the court library, Klosterneuburg monastery (his »Austrian Escorial«), the Karlskirche, the court stables and the Winter Riding School. Joseph Emanuel Fischer von Erlach, architect to the court from 1725, took on the responsibility of completing some of the works begun by his father Johann Bernhard who died in 1723.

The contract for the first building for the Emperor's horses was awarded to Johann Bernhard Fischer von Erlach in 1713. An extensive building was to be constructed for 600 horses and 200 carriages near the glacis in front of the castle gate. The architect, who had already submitted a breathtakingly monumental plan for the Schönbrunn lust and hunting lodge, came up with something very special for this building complex. The ideal plan not only envisaged simple stables and adjoining rooms, but also a giant horse pond as well as a veritable imperial amphitheatre for the court's horse carousels. There was clearly not enough money in the treasury coffers for these bombastic plans, but the court stables (today the Museumsquartier), then built under the supervision of Fischer von Erlach junior, were still amongst the most marvelled royal stables in European seats of residence.

The senior stable master also resided at the court mews – he was the imperial official in charge of all stud farms, the riding schools, the various stables and the carriages of the Habsburg monarchy. In today's parlance, the head stable master had the rank of a minister and the position was therefore always filled by a member of the high aristocracy. The last two head stable masters before the monarchy crumbled in 1919 were Earl Ferdinand Kinsky and Prince Nicolaus Pálffy.
Joseph Richter's *Eipeldauer letters* describe the »Residence where the Emperor's horses live« thus: »Dear Cousin, they have better lodgings than the Emperor himself«.

Eventually in 1729, new court architect Joseph Emanuel Fischer von Erlach submitted plans for a winter riding school to be integrated into the overall complex of the Hofburg. It was to be six years before the »newly constructed and splendidly fabricated imperial riding school« was opened.

THE WINTER RIDING SCHOOL

Opposite page: Emperor Karl VI on a white horse, a Karst from the Spanish stable. This picture is special in many regards as it was created by two painters. The figure of the Emperor in the silver armour is by Johann Gottfried Auerbach; the white horse is the work of Johann Georg Hamilton. This painting is in the court loge and is traditionally saluted by trainers and eleves when entering the arena (above).

The jewel in the crown of this absolute ruler's adornment in the baroque period was, and is, the riding arena, which Emperor Karl VI dedicated to the »aristocratic youth for training and practise as well as for training of horses for artistic riding and war«. This inscription (albeit in Latin) is on the entrance wall of the winter riding school.

Karl VI, horse enthusiast and passionate rider, opened the winter riding school on September 14th 1735 together with his wife and a huge entourage. On view were 54 young stallions brought to Vienna from the imperial stud farms and a number of trained horses. But the real sensation was the riding arena itself – 58 metres in length, 17 metres wide and encircled by a two-storey gallery.

32

The most beautiful riding arena in the world is 58 metres long and 17 metres wide. But the most fascinating is that a magnificent ceiling floats overhead at a height of 17 metres without any supporting columns. This type of free-floating ceiling structure on this scale was an unprecedented innovation in the 18th century.

The column architecture on the long sides of the gallery and the height of 17 metres virtually form a temple to horsemanship which when taken as a whole is a work of great harmony. The two pillars in the middle of the arena were used to train horses. To the eye of the viewer, they are a pleasant breakpoint along the length of the arena but are now contentious as regards the training of animals.

The huge hall does not feature any colour at all – everything is pure architecture which, thanks to the large windows on the long sides (and today's huge crystal chandeliers) glows in a mellow ivory colour. It is only the portrait of the builder in the court loge along the narrow side which introduces colour into the hall. Even today, this famous painting, created by two painters, is much more than just simple wall decoration. When the trainers of the Spanish Riding School enter the riding arena on their Lipizzan stallions, they begin their performance by taking off their tricorns to the portrait of Karl VI. This gesture may now seem a little odd in the 21st century, but by doing so the riders are thanking the builder for the privilege of working in the most beautiful riding arena in the world.

This is where the high nobility once amused themselves – from here members of the imperial family, if not on horses themselves, followed events in the arena. On one side the boxes have windows opening to Michaelerplatz, on the other a door opens to the riding arena of the Winter Riding School. With their very unusual ambience and unrivalled imperial atmosphere, they are a wonderfully representative setting (and available for hire incidentally).

Times and Conventions

Above:
Lavish festivities continue to be held at the Spanish Riding School. Seen here are the preparations for the big fund-raising dinner in autumn 2009 – watched on intently by a stallion.

Opposite page:
Carrousel in the Winter Riding School on January 2nd 1743. Riding on the white horse: Maria Theresia. Painting by Martin van Meytens, 1743 (detail).

ARISTOCRATIC REVELRY

Even under its builder, Karl VI, the Winter Riding School was not only intended to be an exclusive institution for training horses and aristocratic offspring, but also a splendid baroque setting for glamorous celebrations. Especially popular with spectators and those participating were the carousels, a playful advancement of courtly tournaments. These luxuriously laid-in celebrations were held in many places in town streets and squares – for the amusement of their residents. In Vienna, the Winter Riding School was usually the setting for these courtly divertissements. Regulated meticulously in the ceremonial protocols of the court was that no expense or organisational effort was spared for carrousels, lancing the rings and piercing the Moors' heads.

The name »Spanish Riding School« did not become common until the late 18th century. Before it was simply the »Riding School«. From 1789 onwards, the official name of the Winter Riding School was »K. K. Stadtreitschule« (Royal and Imperial City Riding School). The name »Spanish Riding School« actually came from colloquial speech. Since the 16th century, the court stables have been called the »Spanish stable«. From Karl VI onwards in the first half of the 18th century, the imperial riding horses were commonly called »Original Spaniards« or »Spanish variety« horses. The term »Spanish Riding School« was, we can state with a degree of certainty, formed from it – to 1918 more or less unofficially, thereafter officially.

The lead performers were not only the ladies and gentlemen of the gentry, and often their offspring, but also mainly the horses. For this type of entertainment, they had to be trained perfectly such that they allowed themselves to be directed by carriage riders and horse riders with slight movements in tight spaces.

Reigned up in front of small, delicately carved and colourfully painted carriages and sleighs or ridden by deft knights, it was the horses which had the main role. All manner of skills were demonstrated on and with them. The heads of Moors and Turks (not real ones of course) were charged with lances, daggers and also pistols. The aim was to pierce the middle of rings or wreaths with lances or daggers without leaving the set course or missing specified turns. Even the ladies had to adeptly complete certain tasks in the delicate carriages or sleighs, often in unison with their knight. The ladies and gentlemen had specially matching costumes made for these kinds of celebrations and even the horses were adorned with plaits and braids.

It goes without saying that this level of effort was not possible on a day-to-day basis. But the carousels were extremely popular in the Winter Riding School for large events.

Piercing Moors' heads demanded particular dexterity from rider and perfectly drilled horse. Riders had to hit stuffed balls, the Moors' heads, with swords and lances whilst keeping to meticulous cheoreography. Painting by Ignace Duvivier, 1780.

Living tradition – for the Spanish Riding School, this means re-adopting the wonderful custom of large-scale celebrations in the Riding School. For example, noble fund-raising dinners with subsequent auctioning of beloved memorabilia from the Riding School have already been held, and the Winter Riding School will again host glamorous balls in 2010. But the high point will be in summer 2010 with the holding of the *Fête Impériale,* a lavish ball in the best Viennese tradition in which the riding arena becomes a stage of sumptuous robes and hot-blooded dancing couples. So *Trend meets Tradition,* in the truest sense of the word.

But celebrations were not only held on horseback and in carriages at the Winter Riding School. 1744 saw the riding school converted into a magnificent ballroom when a masked ball was held for the marriage of Maria Theresia's younger sister Maria Anna. Simple numbers tell of the splendour – 130 chandeliers were installed and 52 large mirrors reflected the sixty knights and ladies of court society, dressed in the same colour and style, together with the 8000 invited guests.

One of the most magnificent carrousels took place on January 2ⁿᵈ 1743 in the Winter Riding School. The reason was the retreat of French and Bavarian troops from Bohemia after the first Silesian war. In small, delicately carved carriages driven carefully by knights sat ladies whose function it was to guide the lances. In parallel, a complicated quadrille was ridden under the leadership of Maria Theresia herself. The pompous event took place with musical accompaniment. Painting by Martin van Meytens, 1743.

On selected occasions, aristocratic guests and citizens of the city were able to admire the Lipizzans. One such event was the entrance of Isabella of Parma, the bride of Emperor-to-be Josef II, Maria Theresia's son. Painting by Martin van Meytens and his atelier, around 1760/65.

FROM THE VIENNA CONGRESS TO THE END OF THE CENTURY

The Vienna Congress, starting in the autumn of 1814 and sluggishly continuing on to early summer 1815, was a time of lavish festivity. A great deal of money was spent on providing the many invited highest-ranking diplomats distraction from laborious negotiations. 80,000 guilders a day are said to have been diverted from state coffers into the countless celebrations, balls and festivities. »Le congrès ne marche pas, il danse« (»The congress is dancing instead of making progress«), Field Marshal Charles Joseph Fürst von Ligne is said to have commented in resignation.

The Winter Riding School was a popular setting for these celebrations. When required, its riding arena was converted into a concert hall, a palm house or a scented orange garden . The performance of Beethoven's symphonic master-piece *Wellington's Victory* must have been particularly brilliant – a monstrous composition in terms of the orchestra line-up which the master himself conducted.

A new era began with the French Revolution, the end of the reign of Napoleon and the new order of Europe with the Vienna Congress. Elegant celebrations and exquisite delights of course continued to be held at the courts of Europe, but the shine of the Ancien Regime, the time prior to 1800, was finally assigned to the past. Also, the court riding schools in which classic horsemanship was being fostered at the highest standard were disappearing from virtually everywhere in Europe. Only Vienna was different. Here, and nowhere else, the tradition was being kept alive high above the imponderabilites of history.

It was actually the Vienna Congress which pointed the way forward for the Spanish Riding School – as an institution in which classic horsemanship was being fostered on an extremely high level and as visual grandeur being presented to enthusiastic audiences. This imperial riding performance was held in the Winter Riding School in 1814. The eventful, yet harmonical, arrangement was only possible when horse and rider formed a perfectly coordinated unit. Water colour and ink by Johann Nepomuk Hoechle, 1814.

Below:
Crown Prince Rudolf on a stallion showing the Levade.

Even the society of music lovers used the magnificent arena of the Winter Riding School.

The 19th century saw a series of very different events held in the Winter Riding School. For example, a »trade product fair« was held in 1830 and the stock exchange was relocated to the riding arena in 1831. State class lottery draws also took place in the Winter Riding School. In 1843, a rather militaristic carousel of cavalry offices was held and ten years later a lavish carousel to honour the Kings of Prussia and Belgium. In between, in the revolution year of 1848, the Winter Riding School was also the venue of the constituent session of the first Austrian parliament.

The last celebration held on a large scale in line with the principles of Maria-Theresia style rococo took place in April 1894. Dressed in historical costumes, the two hundred or so participants, amongst them 125 riders, played out how Emperor Karl VI brought his bride Elisabeth Christine von Braunschweig-Wolfenbüttel to Vienna. Historical costumes, rider quadrilles and carousels drawn by two and four horses allowed the baroque riding hall in the centre of Vienna to once again radiate in the splendour of a bygone age.

END AND NEW BEGINNING – 1919–1945

There can be no question that the stars of the Spanish Riding School in Vienna have always been the splendid white horses. But behind the scenes there were committed trainers and stable masters who battled against all external factors for the survival of the Court Riding School. Their victories should be the topic of discussion.

One person the Riding School had much to thank for during the transition from the monarchy to the emerging Republic of Austria, and some years beyond, was Rudolf van der Straten.

Morning session in the Winter Riding School. On the extreme left by the posts is senior stable master Prince Emerich Thurn und Taxis training the saddled white horse Pluto Montedora in the capriole. Painting by Ludwig Blaas, 1890.

Spring 1921 saw the first public performance of the white stallions at the Court Riding School in Vienna since the demise of the monarchy. And Rudolf van der Straten did more still. He went on tour with the horses, giving them international fame. In 1925, when the economic hardship of Austria was heading towards its high point, there was a risk that the Court Riding School would be closed for ever. But Van der Straten, thanks to his tirelessness, held a stunning trump in his hand. The Court Riding School had become so popular that intense national and international intervention prevented closure.

He was head stable master under the last two dual monarchy senior stable masters Graf Kinsky and Fürst Pálffy who were devoted to the Lipizzans and the tradition of the establishment. With a number of loyal trainers and senior trainers on his side, he managed to transfer the Spanish Riding School from the monarchy to the Republic.

This was no easy feat because people no longer wanted to know about imperial institutions after the lost war and the end of the monarchy. Final goodbyes had, after all, even been said to the gentry. On the other hand, if such an institution were to carry on, it must also be economically efficient, especially given the precarious economic position of the state. Van der Straten was therefore faced with the task of making it comprehensible to Austrians, using public performances, that retaining the tradition-rich riding school in the old Hofburg was worthwhile. A program otherwise reserved for the pleasure of rulers and monarchs was staged here – horsemanship and music, but this time for people who knew little or nothing of riding or, most notably, the High School.

The challenge had been overcome. What's more, the Ministry of Agriculture, under whose control the Riding School now was and which had appointed Van der Straten as its director, sent him on tour with the Riding School. This was unheard of and had never happened before. But the young, weak Republic had to set about gaining a foothold on the international stage – if that meant with a cultural

Training in the Spanish Riding School for the 1936 Summer Olympics in Berlin. Photo taken on May 28th 1936.

George S. Patton, US Army General, on a Lipizzan stallion. Photograph from around 1944.

legacy from the battered monarchy, then so be it. The tour took in Berlin in 1925, London in 1927, The Hague in 1928 and Brussels in 1932. When the Spanish Riding School was invited back to London with its white stallions in 1935, its popularity internationally, and domestically in Austria, was finally sealed.

Born in Mostar in 1898, Major Alois Podhajsky was an officer in the Austrian army and had already celebrated successes as a show jumper and dressage rider before being assigned to the Riding School in 1934. When the Spanish Riding School was placed under the auspices of the Ministry of Agriculture in Berlin after the »annexation« in 1938, Van der Straten said his farewells and proposed Podhajsky as his successor. Podhajsky, who had won a bronze medal in dressage at the summer Olympics in Berlin in 1936, took up his new post on March 1st 1939.

Podhajsky regarded himself as being under extreme political pressure from the very start – and there was also a threat of war. To protect the school stallions from allied bombing, he moved them from the city centre of Vienna to the old stables of the

Hermesvilla in Lainz zoo. For political reasons, the district National Socialist administration prohibited final evacuation from Vienna before 1945. When it was finally authorised, Podhajsky fled with the stallions to St. Martin bei Schärding in Upper Austria where he was taken in at the Arco family's castle.

In the meantime, the horses were taken from Piber to Hostau in the »protectorate of Bohemia«. Hostau was under the control of the German Armed Forces and during the 1940s it became a collection point for top-class horses from across Europe, including animals from Lipica. When it became clear that the war was finally lost, the entire herd in Hostau (at least a thousand horses) were spirited away in a cloak and dagger operation to the American occupied zone. 215 horses were transferred to Podhajsky

Ladies program during the Chruschtschov-Kennedy summit meeting in June 1961 in Vienna. Jacqueline Kennedy in the Spanish Riding School. Photograph by Barbara Pflaum, 1961.

Opposite page:
Group Captain Alois Podhajsky with a Lipizzan stallion in the Spanish Riding School. Courbette on the long rein. Photograph by Harry Weber, 1955.

who was able to house them in Wimsbach bei Wels where they remained until 1952. Alois Podhajsky leveraged the passion of commander-in-chief of US troops, General George S. Patton, for the High School of horsemanship by putting on a performance for him so he would place »his« Lipizzans and the Spanish Riding School under the protection of the Americans. Podhajsky ensured the survival of the Riding School with this clever tactical chess move.

The situation was fragile however. As a former officer in the armed forces, Podhajsky was at risk of being arrested, the horses were in Upper Austria and he could not even consider returning to Vienna due to the generally precarious supply situation. But slowly the day-to-day routine returned – for the stallions too. They did not appear again at the Winter Riding School, but regular performances were held in Wels. A time of triumphal tours began which saw the first appearance of Lipizzans in the USA in 1950. The horses and their trainers did not return to Vienna until the signing of the Austrian treaty. In their first performance on October 26th 1955 in the Winter Riding School, their celebration of returning to the Hofburg was as touching as it was dazzling.

Podhajsky remained director of the Spanish Riding School until 1964. His era ended with an extremely successful tour of the United States during which the white horses from Vienna and their riders were met with rapturous acclaim.

Group Captain Alois Podhajsky on the day of his retirement, January 8th 1965, in the stallion stables at the Stallburg in Vienna. Photograph by Harry Weber, 1965.

Group Captain Alois Podhajsky with a Lipizzan stallion in the Spanish Riding School. Capriole on the long rein. Photograph by Harry Weber, 1955.

LIPIZZAN STUD PIBER

Above and
opposite page:
The »Kindergarten« of
the Lipizzan stud Piber.

IMPERIAL IDYLL

The Lipizzan horses stud in Piber is well worth a visit. This is where they are, the next generation of famous white stallions of the Spanish Riding School in Vienna. And this is where the foaling mares live, the treasure of the stud. A trip here is also informative. Two small museums, lovingly appointed and with educational exhibits, answer any questions on horses in their roles as mounts and carriage horses. And do not forget the children's cinema! The diversified program of events in the arena in summer also reminds us that the Lipizzans were always used as horses to draw the elegant carriages of rulers.

It is captivating countryside at the foot of the Stubalpe and Gleinalpe – gentle hills in all shades of green, church towers with their baroque domes nestling in-between and small woods with thickly leaved trees. Here, fifty kilometres or so west of state capital Graz, lies Piber, the state stud farm where Lipizzans are born, grow up and later, after long »years of service«, are allowed to enjoy well-deserved retirement.

The St. Lambrecht Benedictine monastery which was first mentioned in the 11th century, was dissolved under Maria Theresia's reform-oriented son, Emperor Josef II. The baroque abbey building with the Arkadenhof, reminiscent of Italy, was converted into a palace and was, from 1798, set up as a military horse stud.

When, at the end of the First World War, the monarchy was history and only a small country was left from the remnants of the once immense multinational state of the Habsburgs, negotiations on splitting up the Lipizzans also took place. The issue was somewhat complicated because the herd of around three hundred horses from Lipica (mares and foals) had been taken to safety during the First World War. Italy had been on the side of the wartime enemy since 1915 and Lipica was therefore no longer safe territory.

Some of the horses from the Trieste Karst were moved to Laxenburg near Vienna, some others to Kladrub near Prague. With the signing of the French peace treaties, these horses were also divided up. In Kladrub (and hence in the possession of Czechoslovakia), every horse taken there remained. Those in Laxenburg had to be split with Italy. The 250 or so trained and draft horses in Vienna remained unaffected by this split. Lastly, 97 mares and foals were granted to Austria.

The brand mark of the Piber Lipizzan stud farm.

Piber turned out to be beneficial for the continued breeding of the Lipizzans and, by adhering to strict breeding criteria, this unique breed has been able to survive.

Today, Piber is a flourishing business whose primary remit is of course the breeding of Lipizzans but which also has substantial agriculture, forests and mountain pastures.

The castle on the knoll houses the administration centre for the Lipizzan stud farm in Piber.

PLACE OF BIRTH

Horse breeding is highly complicated and barely transparent to the layman. The level of responsibility held by the head of the stud farm in Piber, veterinary doctor Dr. Max Dobretsberger, his senior stud master Leopold Weiss and a number of highly qualified employees in the stables and offices, is very high. The principles of genetics, together with the very latest findings, are part and parcel of basic knowledge.

The Piber Lipizzan stud farm essentially fulfils two primary functions. Firstly, the best and most beautiful stallions

A mare is pregnant for 330 days, about eleven months. When the birth is imminent,
she is brought into the birth stable in a spacious stall and cared for round the
clock by experienced and loving carers. Foals are usually born in the quiet hours
of the night when the world is asleep and the mare feels very secure. The
procedure itself is unusually short – barely twenty minutes pass between the first
contraction and the birth of a foal. Horses are flight animals – i.e. nature
has arranged for the birth to be as short as possible. The senior stud master is
usually the attendant at birth. He cuts the umbilical cord and provides the
mother with sustantial substinance.

are bred for the Spanish Riding School. Secondly, the pure and
healthy Lipizzan line must be continued. Breeding in Piber is
currently based upon a herd of about seventy brood mares
organised into seventeen mare families. These seventeen mare
families can be traced back to the 18th century. The »family
founders« introduced first-class foals to the world and were
continued in the stud books. Female foals are still being assigned
to the appropriate mare family today.

A mare foal is guided through »primary school« for five
years in Piber. This includes becoming accustomed to bridles,
lunge and later the bit and harness. Training and fitness are

therefore just as much part of the daily routine for the Lipizzan
ladies as they are for the stallions. The age of four then sees
training with saddle and in a harnessed team. During this time,
the mares are closely watched and their progress, character traits,
physical attributes and condition are documented accurately.

This performance testing is crucial in deciding whether
a young mare is incorporated into the mother herd, i.e. becomes
a »stud mare«. If yes, she is covered for the first time at the age
of five. In the ideal case she gives birth to one foal per year from
this point on. Her foals are of course also subject to detailed
documentation. How does the birth procedure go, how many
foals does she give birth to over the years, how many and which

The foal is able to stand up on its own four legs after just half an hour – a little
wobbly perhaps, and sometimes the initial attempts end up in the soft straw, but it
does not take long for the sense of balance to win out in the end. After so much
work immediately after the birth, the first pangs of hunger are satisfied with
mother's milk. This mare milk is worth its weight in gold because it contains major
nutrients and antibodies which protect the foal from illness during the first few
weeks of its life. This first meal works as a vaccination.

The original stud books, the *Grundbücher des kaiserlichen Hofgestüts (Register of the imperial court stud farm)* can be traced back to the year 1750. It is not known in detail which genetic crosses made up the much-coveted »Spaniards« before this time. But we can say with certainly that the first aristicratic family in Europe, the Habsburg establishment, prefered the »Spanish variety« horses and therefore influenced all European courts and aristocratic estates. Any self-respecting person was breeding Spanish horses from the 16th/17th century. There was barely any talk of individual breeds, as we know them today, until about two hundred years ago. Breeding of Lipizzans in Piber is strictly regulated by federal law and the *Ursprungszuchtbuch* (original stud book).

are trained as young stallions in the Spanish Riding School, how many of her female offspring are integrated into the mother herd. This thorough and meticulous record taking over years produces an invaluable data pool – a priceless basis for breeding in general.

KINDERGARTEN

»New year's baby 2010«. A perfect baby mare, born on January 18th. Her father is one of the most famous trained stallions in Vienna, Favory Amabilia.

When mother and foal move from the birth stable to the pen about a week after the birth, the foal is still dark. It does not get the famous milky-white colour until the age of six to nine years. At least there is a high probability of this. 99 out of 100 foals attain the milky-white colour with one staying brown or black. These are the Sunday children, considered lucky horses, which are also accepted into the Spanish Riding School if they exhibit the appropriate level of quality. Currently there are two, Pluto Bellornata and Favory Aquileja. The fact that Lipizzans are also brown or black as fully

grown horses is not erratic genetic behaviour but old genetic constitution coming through. Up to 200 years ago, Lipizzans were bred in different colours – the milky-white colour was not pursued vigorously for breeding purposes until after this time.

When mother and foal arrive in the pen, socialisation of the young animals begins. This is because only fifty percent of their character and ability they will form is made up from hereditary predispositions – the other half is the consequence of environmental conditions. And there is hardly anywhere else where they are more appropriate to the species than at the Piber stud farm. Careful attention is paid to ensuring the foals play around enough, that they are out and about in the fresh air every day, that they do not overexert themselves when letting off energy, that they drink enough of their mother's milk, eat properly and also get enough rest. It is of course the carers who take care of everything. An important basis for later life is formed in the first few weeks of their existence – the trust of these horses to humans. One reason for their later friend-liness and, above all, docility. The wonderful thing about Lipizzans is that subsequent training is a natural continuation of this animal to human relationship and that also not the slightest physical or psychological distress is inflicted on the horse with the strenuous and demanding training at the Spanish Riding School.

This heaven on earth lasts for six months until the foals are separated from their mothers. The pain is soon overcome. The mares are usually already pregnant again and the foals discover very new challenges in the foal herd.

The names of stallion foals are decided upon before birth. They bare, very nobly, a double-barrelled name made up of the name of the father's line and that of the mother.

Stallion and mare foals still form one herd together – in which somewhat turbulent hierarchies form occasionally. For the human observer at the stud farm, it is of course interesting to see which foals assert themselves as leaders. Conclusions on the attributes to be significant later can be drawn already – strength of character, ability, stamina, couragousness and intelligence.

One year after their birth, the yearlings are separated by gender and integrated into existing young stallion and young mare herds. This is where they meet two and three year old horses and the playing around for rank and dominance starts anew. People are always with them. Carers and managers at the breeding farms provide feed, inspect the hooves and general physical condition and also start with training, such as putting on halters and leading by the hand.

During the course of primary sampling (a big event in the year of the stud farm), it is not only the future trained stallions which are selected. Just as much importance is attached to the selection of young mares. Young mares selected are subjected to performance testing – both in riding and driving, and where applicable incorporated into the herd of foaling mares. Even young stallions not sent to Vienna are trained in Piber in accordance with all the rules of art. Presentations held by the stud farm show how high the quality of this training is. Many horse experts and lovers are thrilled and very glad about what they see, so much so that Lipizzans from Piber are also offered for sale every year.

Above:
Childhood summers spent on the mountain pasture are one reason for the excellent physical constitution of the Lipizzans.

Opposite page:
Lipizzan mares are also readily trainable, plucky and bold – they are broken in and trained for horse-drawn carriages.

The summers spent on local mountain pastures by the young horses represent a particular pleasure during this period. Here, 1600 metres above sea level, where the terrain is often steep, the air is wonderfully clean and the climate sometimes harsh and changeable, and the meadows entice with an abundance of scented herbs, character builds, surefootedness is trained, tendons and joints become elastic and firm in equal measure and heart, circulation, lungs and immune system are strengthened. During this time, lasting from June to the end of August, the horses are continually overseen by their carers, brought into the stable and groomed. To regard humans as partners of a higher social rank is also a major area of learning. An indispensible condition for subsequent training, especially at the Spanish Riding School.

The first step in this direction starts in August when the management of the stud farm arrives on the mountain pasture to subject the young animals to preliminary sampling. Main sampling takes place after the third summer on the mountain pasture in October. Now it is the three-year-old mares and stallions in particular which are subject to precise analysis. Movement disposition, constitution, body size and build, and of course ancestry are the criteria which will be decisive for the animals in years to come. Stallions for the Spanish Riding School are selected jointly by stud farm management, the senior stud farm master, the head of the riding arena and experienced head trainers.

Finally the young stallions move to the Stallburg in Vienna at the age of about three and a half years. What may sound late is perfectly normal for Lipizzans. Compared to other breeds, Lipizzans are »late developers«, but do reach an unusually high age – and remain powerful and robust well into old age. Mares aged over twenty years are no rarity in the mother herd – the oldest Lipizzans live for more than thirty years.

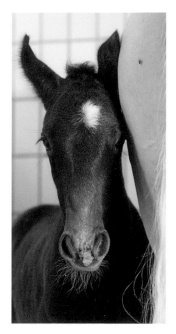

RESIDENCY FOR THE SENIORS

When the most talented young stallions are chauffeured to Vienna in cold January, life begins in earnest. As much as they will prove to be readily trainable in the coming six years or so, and as much as we will admire them in all their grandeur in the Winter Riding School, we also feel sorry for them a little in having to move into the city from the idyllic rolling countryside of Western Styria.

They may return to Piber from time to time during their working life. After all, they are trained stallions and should also bequeath their outstanding qualities. There are therefore annual

trips to the stud farm to bring them together with selected mares as »cover« stallions. Ensuring a balanced family grouping is part and parcel of the remit of the stud farm.

The trained stallions remain at the Spanish Riding School for at least twenty years. Only when it becomes apparent to trainers and carers in Vienna that tiredness is setting in, when the sense is that they have received enough applause and that the shine is slowly fading, may they take their well-deserved retirement.

Now, at the age of about twenty five years, they make their last journey to Piber. Here they are allowed to rest after a long and successful working life, to enjoy the good air and to listen to birds twittering instead of Johann Strauß. They need not train any more, they need not learn any more, but they still receive all the love and devotion. They are cared for and groomed and their health is monitored carefully. And sometimes they get a visitor when their former trainer, with whom he once proudly performed routines in the Winter Riding School, has a yearning to see his old colleague. Lipizzan stallions are guaranteed a good and friendly retirement in Piber.

One of the most famous »retirees« in Piber was Siglavy Beja. Born in 1964, the stunningly beautiful white stallion was one of the very top stars at the Spanish Riding School up to the age of 27. Six years after his retirement, the father of 99 foals was given the opportunity of once again captivating the audience when he was invited into the arena as part of the gala to celebrate the 200 year anniversary of Piber. The years had taken a slight toll on the old man, the musculature was no longer as taut but the posture was as first-class as ever. Siglavy Beja accepted the standing ovations graciously and with elegant *Grandezza*. Two weeks later, almost 35 years of age, he died. Later the word would be that Siglavy Beja had been waiting for this last brilliant appearance.

THE FINE ART OF RIDING

Above:
Work on the long rein
– a challenge for the
power of concentration
of horse and rider.

Opposite page:
Airs above ground are
performed under the
rider and without stirrups
at the Spanish Riding
School. The seating
position is lower and
hence the bond between
horse and rider more
intense. This always
requires that the rider
is seated perfectly and
has absolute balance.

The rediscovered antiquity

To comprehend how much stamina and discipline is necessary before a Lipizzan, and with it the trainer, is »ready for the stage« (because the High School is about the training of horse and person), we need to take a brief foray into history. This is because the High School of horse dressage has a long tradition.

The centuries in a nutshell: It begins in the antiquity with Xenophon whose credits and works have already been discussed at the beginning. Some 2000 years later (the time around 1500), the recollection in the epoch of Renaissance is of the antiquity whose architecture, literature and sculpturing one wanted to revitalise just as much as the knowledge of horse breeding and horsemanship.

One of the first people to use the old teachings in a contemporary manner and to record them in a famous book was Neapolitan riding instructor Federico Griso, who appointed the director of the first modern European riding school, Giovanni B. Pignatelli, to his institute. Griso's book *Gli ordini di cavalcare* was published in 1552 and anybody reading it now will wonder which crude means were used by Griso to train young horses. Griso's understanding of the sole of a horse was more on the minimal side, although we also need to know that the Neapolitaner was a pretty stroppy horse which was not easy to train. Nevertheless, Griso's work is regarded as the first purposefully methodical canon for the training of horse and rider.

However, the purpose of this riding lesson was not to develop a kind of self-sufficing art form. It was more a matter of training

> **The small dictionary of the High School**
> *Throughness:* A horse is *through* when it responds sensitively to the finest of aids from its trainer. The hind legs of a horse precisely following the hoof prints of the front legs is said to be *simple hoof print*. The back legs of a horse are called *hindquarters* and the front legs *forehand*. The *point of contact* is when the hooves touch the ground – when walking, on the same side but not at the same time (four hoofbeats can be heard), when trotting, the diagonal leg pairs always touch the ground one just after the other (two hoofbeats can be heard) and when galloping, three hoofbeats can be heard – first the outer hind leg, then the inner hind leg and the outer foreleg simultaneously, lastly the inner foreleg. *Haunches* denote the hip, stifle and hocks of horses, gymnasticised purposefully for *haunch bending*. Perfect, powerful haunch bending is essential for the High School as it guarantees perfect balance by improved the positioning of the hindquarters underneath the horse. Also associated with the horse »treading« is the *collection* in which, when the haunches are bent slightly, pressure is relieved from the hindquarters and thrust is converted into load capacity.

the rider well enough so that he was well aware of the abilities of the horse and was able to control and use them at any time. In tournaments, in the riding school, for parades and for representation, and above all in the battles of war.

Giovanni Pignatelli's and Federico Griso's teachings were continued by three French riding masters – Salomon de la Broue, Chevalier de Saint-Antoine and, in particular, Antoine de Pluvinel. Pluvinel, a student of Pignatelli's and riding instructor for the later French king Louis XIII, recorded his principles in *Instruction du Roi en l'art de monter à Cheval*. He first recommended the posts to keep the horse in place, and the bitless bridle for working with the horse when leading it by the hand.

The 17th century saw a few publications appear on horsemanship, also in Germany where the dedication was to the art of war on horseback – both in practise and in theory. It was not until the 18th century that a genius again appeared on the stage of the High School. François Robichon de la Guérinière. The senior stable master at the court of King Louis' XV wrote the, in the truest sense of the word, epochal work *École de Cavalerie* in which he not only propagated a modern, sleek type of riding seat, but also the so-called »shoulder-in«, a key movement in classic High School.

The last two theoretic/methodic principles for the High School at the Spanish Riding School ultimately originated from three of its senior trainers.

Illustrations from the *Encyclopédie* of Denise Diderot and Jean Baptiste d'Alembert. Croupade (above), capriole (below) and piaffe between the posts (very bottom).

In 1898, Berlin-born Franz Holbein von Holbeinsberg, together with Maximilian Weyrother and Johann Meixner, wrote the *Directiven für die Durchführung des methodischen Vorganges bei der Ausbildung von Reiter und Pferd in der k. u. k. spanischen Hofreitschule (Instructions for performing the methodic procedure in the training of horse and trainer at the royal and imperial Spanish Riding School)*, and Alois Podhajsky's *Die klassische Reitkunst (Classic Horsemanship)* is still regarded as a principle work in dressage riding.

They are all applicable – Xenophon who recognised the mentality of the horse like virtually no other, Griso, to whom we can at least take our hats off to as a pioneer, Pluvinel and La Guérinière, who made considerable progress in the High School, and finally the »Viennese« riding instruction of Holbeinsberg, Weyrother, Meixner and Podhajsky.

But all this remains grey theory compared to the most intensive school for rider eleves and young stallions which ultimately makes them masters of their art – the verbal passing on of Senior Rider's practical knowledge from generation to generation.

PRACTISE, PRACTISE, PRACTISE!

When we see in the performances of the Spanish Riding School the perfect harmony between rider and horse in no less perfect choreography, everything seems to be all a matter of course. But behind this perfection are years of work, daily training and endless patience.

Everything begins with the arrival of the young stallions from Piber. They are selected in a meticulous, protracted procedure in Piber, are three and a half years

Opposite page:
The training and gymnasticising of stallions are tailored to the talent of every individual animal, recognisable early on. This work is refined over time, resulting in perfectly trained specialisation. This is because not every horse is born to jump courbettes or caprioles.

Below:
Group Captain Alois Podhajsky (standing) training in the Spanish Riding School. Photograph, 1958.

Training session on the
long rein. These exercises
require a high degree of
throughness from the
horse.

old and small children on
four legs – happy, frolic-
some and a kind of *tabula
rasa* in regard to any sort
of dressage training. But
every one of these stallions
has the potential to become
a first-class specialist athletic, a truly great trained
stallion.

Those in the know
can sense very early on the
talent a young, untrained stallion is hiding. It starts with the
young horses being allowed to run around freely in
the riding arena in front of the team of trainers.
They identify very quickly what the coltish animals
have in them. If, for example, one is sensitive and
ticklish and jumps up in the air with all four legs on
the slightest of touches, the assumption is that he
will thrill his audience with exquisite caprioles. Others
on the other hand react to everything and everyone
by climbing up powerfully on their hind legs. In five
to six years time, they are likely to captivate spectators
with elegant courbettes.

But this point is still a long way off. Besides
the assessment of the physical condition, the mental
constitution of the stallions, still dark grey in colour,
is monitored carefully. Many are unable to contain themselves

About one in a hundred.
Not all Lipizzan stallions
attain the milky-white
colour. But if a dark
stallion proves to be
talented, it is accepted
into the Spanish Riding
School despite its »non-
conformant« appearance.
This is because dark Lipizzans are traditionally
regarded as lucky horses.

A young stallion – recog-
nisable by its grey coat –
during a training session.

and their temperament,
many in the group are
alpha animals, many are
patient and friendly, many
react quickly and angrily
and many exercise patience
to everyone and everything.
And just as the physical
virtues and talents are
trained and deployed, the
trainers also use psycho-
logical disposition. Just as

Training sessions in the Winter Riding School. A trained stallion in the piaffe between the posts and the perfect levade is practised in the foreground. On the extreme left is an apprentice on a stallion, led on the lunge by a Senior Rider. A strict rule applies for the riding arena – access only for those on four legs or those on two legs with a uniform!

a spirited stallion is able to infect all other horses, a quiet, perhaps even modest horse is able to calm a whole group. A quiet horse is also docile, and later, when it is trained, can help its human colleagues by, for example, unhurriedly carrying (in the truest sense of the word) a young trainer with stage fright through a first performance.

Intensive training starts with *straightline riding (Remonte training)* in all gaits – i.e. walk, trot and gallop. This way the horse learns to find its balance, to carry a rider on its back and to take initial assistance and instructions from the rider.

The targeted training of all muscle groups begins with the *Campagne school.* Leg and back muscles are strengthened and the thrust of the hind legs trained. Then slow lateral movements, collection, turns and rounds are practised.

The *Haute École* is not started until the third phase of training. Now the trainer who has brought the horse this far ascertains whether the ability and willingness to learn can be cultivated further – whether the horse has this »extra potential« in it which perhaps can make it a star of the Spanish Riding School. If yes, intensive training in the High School starts, and if the horse is a particularly talented, physically powerful and strong-minded stallion, also in airs above ground.

Experienced Senior Riders are able to identify the special talent of their future trained stallions by just watching them romping around.

It is a mixture of encouragement and requirement – and always with regard to the basic disposition of the horse. These gymnastic routines are performed slowly, thoroughly, cautiously and with no pressure to perform and last about six years – until the young stallion has become a trained stallion.

The High School can be regarded as a kind of refinement of nature, as a taming and cultivation of the fundamental mannerisms and natural gaits of the horse. This is because the gaits and jumps of trained stallions are nothing which go against their nature.

The gaits of the High School

To really enjoy a performance at the Spanish Riding School or when watching a supposed leisurely morning workout, it is helpful to disclose the secrets of the High School – or at least the basics.

We already know that the maxim »practise, practise, practise« applies for horses, trainers and would-be trainers and that correct and efficient gymnasticising of the horse and its natural disposition are the prerequisites for the High School. But where does it all lead? What are the elaborate figures the horses perform called? And which unfamiliar traditions, if any, do individual gaits hide?

As a rule of thumb, one can say that the High School, whose foundations as we know were formulated in the Renaissance period, was not merely about *L'art pour l'art*. In fact there were always several aspects to dressage training of horse and rider. Also amongst these over the centuries was having the horse, as a member of a horseback army in battles, safely under control.

Many gaits, be they on or above ground, are practised under the rider and by hand and brought to perfection over the years. *Airs on the ground* are, as the term implies, without jumps, those *above the ground* are highly complex figures in which the horse stands up balancing on its hindquarters or actually performs a jump. It is airs above ground in particular which demand from rider and horse perfect body control, absolute balance and hence a maximum degree of underlying talent – trained to perfection over many years of uninterrupted practise.

AIRS ON THE GROUND

Shoulder-in: This is a key exercise for everything subsequent because the shoulder-in prepares the horse for relieving pressure from the forehand by moving the hindquarters further underneath its body. The shoulder-in is essentially a stepover of the inner forehand over the outer – a simultaneous forwards and sideways movement – from which ultimately all lateral movements in dressage develop.

Half-pass: In this movement, the horse moves forwards and sideways with two hoof beats and is turned around the inner haunch.

Passage or Spanish step: This elegant gait is only performed under the rider and is considered a derivation of the natural display behaviour of a stallion. It is a trot in which the forearms of the horse are raised almost horizontally and the hindquarters must take considerable weight. This delays the speed of movement – the horse poises in time with the rhythm.

Piaffe: This is a type of trot in place or, at the very most, gaining one hoof's width. The hindquarters are lowered noticeably to be able to take the horse's weight. The forehand provides cushioning whilst the diagonal leg pairs touch the ground in place.

Pirouette: The old riding masters called this precarious move »cavorting around on the size of a plate«. In the collected gallop, the trained stallion jumps as small a circle as possible in six to eight jumps without gaining any room. The exercise looks particularly elegant when rhythmically fluent and with beautiful balance.

Levade: With the entire weight on the hindquarters and with heavily bent haunches, the horse lifts its forehand and body at an angle of about 35 degrees. One variation of the Levade is the Pesade in which the horse stands at a greater angle and the hornches are not bent as much.

Courbette: This is also a jump, but the power involved is now immense – because the horse performs several jumps forward on the hindquarters without putting the forehand down on the ground. A masterpiece for trained stallion and rider!

No Time for Idleness

Above:
On the way to morning training at the Winter Riding School.

Opposite page:
Each individual trained stallion has its own saddle, snaffle bit and of course »gold bridle« for perform-ances. The stable master ensures that the bronze plates always have a perfectly polished shine.

Daily work routine
between stables and tack room

The Spanish Riding School is an establishment with perfect organisation throughout at the heart of which lies, and this is what is so fascinating, the highly sensitive creatures on four legs. It is the Lipizzan stallions around which everything is centred here and which are treated with every conceivable care. And this is so from the very first day they spend in Vienna as young, untrained stallions.

It all starts in the stables, whose professional organisation lies in the hands of the stable master. Hannes Hamminger, the

For the daily routine in the stables to run smoothly, the stable master, with the aid of organisation plans compiled on a weekly basis, oversees a number of horse carers and the young eleves who must work in the stable and in the tack room to learn and understand all of the procedures in the background. In addition to these are a few apprentices who are part students at a technical college for horse husbandry and part students at the University of Veterinary Medicine.

stable master, is responsible for everything – the arrangment
of horses in stables, the feeding of horses, the grooming equipment, the tack room, the repairing of saddles and bridles and
much more.

But it is mainly the stable master who knows every individual horse, its preferences and its sensitive points, its moods
and its lovable traits. If all 73 stallions at the Spanish Riding
School were to be all mixed up into a paddock, the herd would
be a collection of individuals to the stable master who could
name all of them without a moment's pause. This is important
because just the arrangement of horses in the stable requires a
high degree of this bond. Nothing is left to chance here and everything is decided according to the characteristic nature of the
animals. Inquisitive horses, for example, are given corner stalls
so they can see as much as possible. Patient stallions are placed
next to alpha animals, extrovert next to introvert – some pass
on temperament to others whilst some others convey a sense of
calm to »colleagues«. After all, thriving cohabitation between

Particularly curious
Lipizzan stallions get
their own »cinema«.
They stand in the new
outside stalls where they
have a view of the whole
yard at the Stallburg. Here
they can see who is com-
ing and who is going, and
they are able to greet,
excitedly and somewhat
vocally, the new arrival
from Styria when intro-
duced to the stable
community.

Anyone having a particular bond with a Lipizzan stallion can adopt a horse or foal. This entails an annual subscription which is earmarked for a particular horse. As a sponsor, you are of course allowed to visit the horse from time to time and, mainly during morning work hours and performances, monitor the progress of your charge. Sponsorships are available to individuals as well as companies.

individual animals means good energy management, which in turn results in excellent training and schooling results.

Young stallions must be introduced to this sensitive habitat every year. When they come from Piber in the winter, they may only initially take neighbouring stalls because they have spent their first years of their lives together in a paddock in Piber. After a period of accustomisation (on both sides since the older horses must first accept the young ones), they are integrated into the community of »white gentlemen«. Then it is off to work and the »boys«, as they are affectionately known, are assigned their final stalls. This is a task which never becomes routine but instead always presents a certain challenge.

There are currently 73 stallions in the stables in Vienna. Given the fact that the stables in the Hofburg can not be extended, this number has remained more or less constant. 2010 will see considerable changes because a riding arena has been complete on the Heldenberg near Klein-wetzdorf, in the Weinviertel in Lower Austria, where the stallions have been spending their holidays. Whereas young stallions previously had to be restricted to four or five per year, there is now the opportunity to train up to fifteen stallions, and from the second or third »school year«, the best can be selected for the Spanish Riding School.

Allocating the sensitive animals the right carers is another delicate task for the stable master. Sometimes, however, the stable master is relieved of this task up to a point – namely when a carer comes requesting a particuar horse. The relationship to the father of the young stallion is often a happy one and so it also makes sense to take the son under custodial care.

The carer of every stallion knows exactly what the charge likes and needs and what it can not stand. Three shifts are

The young stallions are used to nature and large paddocks when they arrive from Piber. As a sweetener for adjustment to life in the stables, they are allowed to enter the riding arena as often as possible in the first few weeks and to run and move around unhindered.

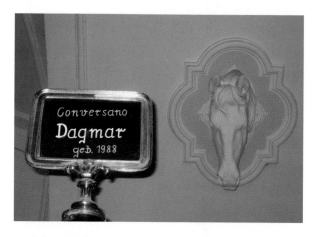

worked – not only to feed, to groom and to clean the stalls, but also to confront any eventuality, to provide comfort when harmony is disrupted a little, to provide encouragement when a tired day lies ahead, to talk to the horses, to give them tender loving care. A team of horse whisperers is at work here!

But the hippophile Menage à trois is not complete without the trainer. This is because the trainer, albeit in a different way, is just as responsible for a horse as the carer. The trainer also often visits the stables and takes care of the horse when not training or performing. So the decision as to which trainer or aspirant trainer is to train a stallion is one which is taken very seriously by the stable master and the manager of the riding arena. After all, given this relationship lasts two decades or so, it should be as harmonious as possible. It is symbiotic communities which evolve here – the life's work of every trainer is »their« trained stallions.

Every carer takes five to six horses under their wing. They feed, clean and groom, check the hooves, monitor the general condition of their charges, check the horses are eating enough, check whether digestion is working as it should and whether the stalls are as clean as they should be. The shift of the main carers starts at six in the morning and carries on to half past two in the afternoon. The bond between carer and horse is intimate. When a young stallion appears for the first time, it is virtually a certainty that its carer is watching on full of pride and is keeping all fingers crossed for the debutant.

EARLY RISERS

The working day of stallions and trainers, aspirant trainers and eleves on the rota begins early. At seven o'clock in the morning, the first group of stallions trots out of the stalls in the Stallburg with their carers towards the Winter Riding School. On most days, there are only three hours before the first visitors arrive for the morning session, open to the public.

Around 40 tons of feed, 120 tons of straw and 140 tons of hay, also carrots, linseed and concentrated feed (pegus pellets). None of this can be stored and must be delivered fresh (for quality reasons alone). The stable master keeps track of the logistics.

Stable master, vet, trainer and carer very carefully decide on the feed for horses. The selection takes into account the temperament and general physical constitution of the animals. What the horses get to eat (exactly three times a day) is shown on the doors of the stalls. On the menu is muesli of the highest quality and of course carrots, linseed (good for a shiny coat) and from time to time sugar lumps (given in moderation to the stallions by riders and carers to keep up the friendship). Two innovations introduced some time ago by Hannes Hamminger are particularly beneficial to the health of the horses. Firstly the stallions are given Grander water to drink, and secondly the hay is energised and vitalised with effective microorganisms.

The tack room is a real treasure trove. This is where bridles and saddles for training and performances hang – some in classic dark brown, some in elegant white deerskin. Every saddle bears the name of the stallion for which it is used. Saddles are readjusted if, during the training period, the muscle structure of the horse changes and the animal becomes more powerful. Much of the equipment is expensive custom design (because much in Vienna is unique), including for example very special dressage snaffle bits whose mouthpieces are softer than usual. Everything is repaired if it can be. Some bridles in the tack room of the Spanish Riding School are up to fifty years old. Excellent material quality is one thing, careful maintenance of all this equipment is another. This also falls under the responsibility of the stable master.

Every training level of eleve, aspirant trainer and, above all, stallion must be satisfied. And because gymnasticising after basic training and remonte and campagne training only bring the required results when performed thoroughly and regularly, a balanced training plan is the be all and end all of successful training, and later down the line, every performance.

Every phase of training needs its space in the riding arena and its time for the work routine. For years, eleves practise perfect seat positioning on the horse when on the lunge. On the other end of the lunge is the trainer who gives these newest members of the team instructions and corrects the posture. Also in need of time are aspirant trainers who are training their first stallions and who are possibly not yet as accomplished as their older colleagues and occasionally transfer their nervousness to their horses.

The trained stallions must also be put through

their paces. A trainer, senior trainer or the manager of the riding arena rides six to seven of them during the course of a working day. But there are moments of uncertainty even in the hands of these experienced riders. The milky-white stars are subject to mood swings just like us humans. There are lethargic days, nervous days and those on which simply nothing gets going.

But these are exceptions. Spectators are able to see how eager training can be by watching morning sessions. Training with the majestic four-legged athletes is open to the public for two hours, usually five days a week. The atmosphere is more informal than for performances. Trainers not riding horses sit on ground level and watch their colleagues intently. The horses are ridden for half an hour, airs on and above ground are practised and then the horses are changed over. Eleves and carers stand ready to throw covers over the sensitive horses so that they do not catch a chill.

The horses are returned to the stables after being exercised. Before marching fully contented into their stalls, they are allowed to

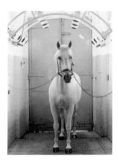

This trained stallion is enjoying the heat lamps after a strenuous training session (above). A regulated working day does not necessarily mean lacklustre routine – quite the contrary in fact for the Spanish Riding School. This is because here the framework of regulations means the highest degree of harmony and reliablity for the principle performers, the Lipizzan stallions. For example, regular grooming does not only mean cleaning of the coat, it also means a pleasant massage for the muscles and intimate contact between animal and person. The same applies for inspection of the hooves and general inspection of the animal.

lounge under heat lamps. This is good for the muscles as it stimulates blood circulation and prevents sore muscles after an intensive training session. It would also appear good for the mind – anyone who has seen a Lipizzan underneath a heat lamp knows what a horse looks like when completely relaxed.

It is impossible to exercise the 73 stallions every day in the riding arena. To preempt a potential lack of exercise, an impressive horse exercise area in the inner courtyard of the Riding School was constructed thanks to generous sponsoring from the private sector. This exercise area (the construction of which required all the powers of persuasion to convince the Hofburg administration and the Office for the Prevention of Historic Monuments) is Europe's largest – and this has one very special benefit. Thanks to the track length of 132 metres, there are relatively long, straight passages which do wonders for the backs and necks of the horses. Exercise areas are usually smaller and form circles, meaning the horse being exercised must always bend its back. The Summer Riding School is located inside the oval of the exercise area. This means visitors to the cafe at the Spanish Riding School can always take pleasure in watching the animals at work in summer.

FROM ELEVE TO SENIOR RIDER

Providing the stallions a perfectly balanced program of exercise and rest is a question of meticulous organisational planning. The manager of the riding arena, Ernst Bachinger, is responsible for this in conjunction with the stable master.

It is of course not only the stallions already trained which undergo training. It is the young stallions in particular which must be trained – and with them the eleves and aspiring trainers. These in turn do not only work with the horses assigned to them, but always under the strict supervision of an experienced trainer.

The training to become a trainer at the Spanish Riding School is unique and prolonged. Young men, and now also young women, start at the age of about fifteen to twenty. Ideally they are able to at least sit on a horse, but are not riders with many years' experience. This is because bad habits could have formed with respect to seating position and contact with the horse which would have to be painstakingly ironed out. Given that the drop-out rate is not inconsiderable, applicants having completed schooling or an apprenticeship are preferred.

Even after ten years, the time from eleve to becoming an aspirant trainer and then trainer, the members of the team are actually still at the beginning of the mastery. Not until two to three horses are fully trained does a trainer feel the sense of being master of his or her craft.

A fundamental innovation – and yet not. The team at the Spanish Riding School has been a male domain for many decades. Although in the era of Maria Theresia, the ladies of the court and the nobility of course took part in the carrousels and passionate rider Empress Elisabeth without doubt used the Winter Riding School, the end of the monarchy has seen only men ride horseback on the Lipizzan stallions in Vienna. In autumn 2008, two apprentices were accepted for the first time – one has stayed and is regarded as a great hope along with her young male colleagues. Training to mount elegantly without stirrups is a hard lesson for all apprentices.

Once an applicant is accepted as an eleve, this is the start of strenuous training which lasts four to six years depending on dedication and talent. In this time eleves must carry out their duties in the stables, tend to saddles and bridles, work on correct seat position on the horse and learn to mount without stirrups. During all of this they are of course under the constant supervision of the stable master on the one hand and the trainer and manager of the riding arena on the other. Following this basic training is the first big hurdle – assessment and the decision as to whether the eleve has managed to become an aspirant trainer.

Another six to eight years follow as kind of apprentice to the riding arena – every aspirant trainer now gets his/her own horse to be trained. Here the aspirants work closely with experienced senior trainers. Knowledge is now combined with riding ability and the skill to communicate it to the stallions. Required in these years as an aspirant trainer is no longer just discipline (this is now assumed), but also a high degree of empathy towards the stallion for which the aspirant assumes responsibility.

It is not until eight to ten years after young riders join the Spanish Riding School as eleves that they get the opportunity to be appointed trainer. A responsible job, because trainers are the bearers of a very old and yet very much alive tradition upheld not least by oral tradition, by the ability to communicate knowledge gained to the next generation. This way the school characterises the trainer and, to the same degree, every individual trainer characterises the school.

The tours of the Spanish Riding School, taking in European countries and those on the other side of the Atlantic, present an organisational challenge of a special kind. Adapted horse transporters with video monitoring, air suspension and special flooring to protect the stallions' joints are used for travelling around Europe. The horses are flown if the tour takes in the USA or Canada, usually on two different scheduled flights with the horses housed in the rear, enclosed part. The stallions master flying with accustomed aplomb. It is also the responsibility of the stable master to ensure that deerskin saddles, gold bridles, snaffles and bridle bits as well as covers and spares/repair material are available in sufficient quantities. Ninety large tour boxes hold everything from riders' uniforms to dubbin. Straw and hay is pre-ordered – one to two tons a week. Only the special muesli is taken with them from Vienna.

DEERSKIN AND COMBED YARN

Trainers are just as elegant as their horses. The uniforms they wear during morning sessions and especially for performances have a long tradition. They originate from the 19th century and are actually working clothes made up of several parts.

Besides the working clothes described here, each trainer also has a uniform jacket and a summer uniform. Trainers slip into their red gala uniforms for special occasions and when instructed by the manager of the riding arena.

Uniform tailcoat

The uniform tailcoat is cut from coffee-brown Trevira combed yarn. The high-necked garment has two rows of six brass buttons on the breast, with a further two on the arms and two on the rear seam. The left coattail hides a pocket for sugar.

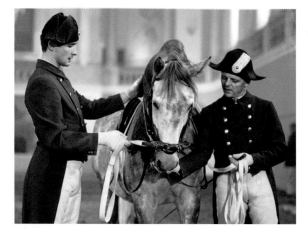

Jodhpurs

The tailor-made jodhpurs are waistband trousers made of white deerskin. The slits in the left and right of the waist band and a two-part belt sewn onto the front of the trousers which can be closed at the back ensure perfect fit of the deerskin jodhpurs. The trousers have stretch bands so that they do not ride up inelegantly or slide at the ankles. White full-grain deerskin is used for the trainers' gloves.

Two-peaked hat

Positions within the team can be identified from the 20 cm long, 40 cm wide and 15 cm high two-peaked hats worn by trainers (in fact from the golden braid attached with a golden uniform button and running diagonally across the two-peaked hat). The golden braid of senior riders and trainers is 3.5 cm wide, that of aspirant trainers 1.5 cm and the narrowest (1 cm) belongs to eleves.

Only the moiré rosette underneath the golden band has the same size, 10 cm. The two-peaked hat is lined with black or white silk and is worn width-wise.

Jackboots
The »Zauber der Montur« continues with elegant, high black leather boots with the front part pulled up. A leather spur sits on the 10 cm high back of the boot lined with brown leather.

Spurs
Chrome-plated steel, a two-part black leather spur strap and a neck length of 4.5 cm are the main parts of the swan-neck spurs which are also a standard part of the service uniform. The team's *whips* are simple birch rod, cut by the trainers themselves on their traditional trip to the Vienna Woods.

HOLIDAY TIME

When summer starts and the whole world goes on holiday, it is also time for the Lipizzan stallions at the Spanish Riding School to take some time off. Since 2005, they have been taken to the Heldenberg in Kleinwetzdorf at the end of June, beginning of July. Here, in the friendly rolling countryside of the Lower Austrian Weinviertel, the stars from Vienna are offered everything the heart desires for a proper holiday – meadows, sun, grass and fresh air.

The countryside is also ideal for exercise training which the horses can only get here – horse riding in the open expanse. Early every morning sees four to six trainers arrive from Vienna. Each of them rides three of four stallions for about an hour.

The rolling countryside, the forest tracks, the meadow paths – a perfect scenic cocktail ensuring that the muscles, tendons and joints of the animals are also trained and rested in equal measure during the holidays.

Riding in the woods on the Heldenberg.

The horses are also attended to here by their carers who travel from the Winter Riding School to Kleinwetzdorf every morning with a company bus. This adds variation to the accustomed, again benefiting the equilibrium of the sensitive animals.

The stallions have a six-week holiday and mid-August sees them return to Vienna. Then the daily training starts anew which visitors are able to watch in the publically accessible morning sessions. The first performance is then scheduled again for the end of August.

But the Winter Riding School does not stand empty in July either. This is because the young ones and mothers come to Vienna from Piber whilst the stallions are on holiday. A special program is laid on six times a week as part of »Piber meets Vienna«. This is where the foals romp around in the arena where normally the stallions perform their complicated routines. Unimpressed by the Emperor's portrait gazing down earnestly from the centre loge (which would normally be saluted respectively), the wild young stallions try to cement their position in the herd. And the mares demonstrate their ability working in harnessed teams.

Opposite page above:
The paddock stalls, so-called »open stables«, are a special set-up at the Heldenberg enabling the horses to enjoy the fresh air in quiet times. Because there are only a certain number of these paddock stalls, a kind of democratic exchange system is in place. Every horse is allowed to stay a while in the paddock stall before swapping with its neighbour so that it also has the chance to see the world outside. It was astonishing for the stable master, who of course also looks after the stallions here, to see how well the animals accepted these open stables. After all, they are accustomed to spending the whole year in enclosed stalls. Yet the horses feel so at home on the Heldenberg that they even sleep outside.

Stars on the Stage

Above:
Piaffe between the posts.

Opposite page:
Schoolquadrille

Elegance and harmony

The high point for horses and trainers is of course performing to an attentive audience – something learned in long, intensive and thorough training. The performances at the Spanish Riding School, featuring all of the finesses of the High School in the Winter Riding School, are amongst the most beautiful and elegant in Vienna. But every spectator should bear in mind that these are not machines but living creatures who, like us, experience different tempers and moods. This means that performances at the Spanish Riding School are always exquisite and to a certain degree perfect – and yet every one is different to the previous one in minor detail. This is because Lipizzan stallions are always graceful – they simply prefer occasionally to get up to something they should not.

A warm-up or »breaking in« of the horses before performances is not necessary. The animals are so excellently trained and have the famous, stalwart character that they walk calmly and disciplined more or less immediately. This is where the slow and

thorough training pays off because the work performed by
the horses during a two-hour or so performance is streneous.
The performances are very exhausting for both trainers and
Lipizzans. The secret is not noticing this effort in either of them.

A trained stallion makes one appearance per performance.
More is not expected of the animals. This means every trainer
who is part of three program events for example, enters the arena
with three horses in every performance. Besides, the stallions
are highly qualified specialists –
some in airs on the ground, some
in airs above the ground and some
others again in precision – a pre-
requisite in the school quadrille.

The stallions are sensitive
beings which pick up on every
mood of their trainers and instantly
those in the arena. During training,
a trainer having a bad day can
pass a horse onto an eleve or aspirant
trainer and watch on for a while
so as not to negatively influence
any four-legged colleagues. This
of course will not do when a performance is imminent – here
physical self-discipline is the order
of the day!

Levade, in-hand

FROM THE YOUNG STALLIONS TO THE SCHOOLQUADRILLE

It starts with the first program event, the young stallions, currently in the first and second year of training. Encouraged by the
applause and the exciting atmosphere, one of the bubbly young
stallions may get ideas which it also shows off – infecting the others
in the process. It is a particularly likeable program event and an
exciting one because it is never possible to predict just what any
»pubescent lad« is likely to think up.

Capriole under the rider.

The proceedings become more serious afterwards. Now the trained stallions enter the arena with their respective routine and perform all gaits and airs of the High School.

Overall it is a harmonic production with music by Mozart, Schubert and Strauß in which every trainer demonstrates individual airs with their athletic specialists. A synchronuous »danced« Pas de Deux is just as much part and parcel of it as pirouettes and formation. Piaffes, passages and half-passes are performed.

One of the high points of course is the performance of the »School above the Ground«, with levades, courbettes and caprioles. They are demonstrated under the rider and on the long rein.

The latter is a particularly special experience telling of the close intimacy between trainer and horse. In the »Gaits on the long Rein«, the trainer goes behind the horse and directs it only with rein and softly spoken aids. The Lipizzan stallion and trainer show high levels of concentration. The horse's ears are pointed alertly backwards towards the trainer and the horse responds to the slightest change in tug direction of the rein.

Page 106|107:
Pas de Deux

It goes without saying that only stallions which are particularly gifted and which have been fostered in this talent in highly sensitive training perform with the long rein.

Another highlight, the closing performance, is the school quadrille, choreography reminiscent of baroque horse ballets. The airs of classic dressage are performed with absolute precision by at least eight horses and their trainers in short lines. The school quadrille lasts about twenty minutes and is therefore, as the longest program event, a challenge to stamina and concentration.

Schoolquadrille

Saluting the portrait of the Emperor in the loge.

Appendix

Above:
Tack room

Opposite page:
The inner courtyard of the
Stallburg – magnificently
decorated and with
removable roof for a large
dinner.

Bibliography – Selection

Gerhard Kapitzke: *Das Pferd von A–Z.* Munich–Vienna, 2003

Georg Kugler. *Lipizzaner. Spanische Hofreitschule. Lipizzaner Museum.* Vienna–Graz–Klagenfurt, 2007

Alain Laurioux|Guilleaume Henry: *Die Schulen der Reitkunst. Wien, Saumur, Jerez, Lissabon.* Schwarzenbek, 2009

Sylvia Loch: *Dressur mit leichter Hand.* Munich–Vienna, 2002

Tomáš Míček: *Habsburgs weiße Hengste.* Stuttgart, 1990

Alois Podhajsky: *Spanische Hofreitschule.* Vienna, 1941

Wolfgang Reuter: *Lipizzaner und Spanische Reitschule.* Innsbruck, 1983

Hanne Schneider|Stephan Hutt: *Lipica.* Stuttgart, 2004

Cordial thanks

to the teams of the Spanish Riding School and the Lipizzan stud Piber: Barbara Sommersacher, Eva-Maria Schöbinger, Ernst Bachinger, Johannes Hamminger, Ines Hubinger and Max Dobretsberger for their time, patience and assistance.

APA/picturedesk.com/Barbara Gindl: 98 b

APA/picturedesk.com/Wilfried Gredler-Oxenbauer: 85

APA/picturedesk.com/Hans Klaus Techt: 91 b

HOFMOBILIENDEPOT: 42 c

IMAGNO/Austrian Archives: Umschlagvorderseite, 8, 9, 14, 15, 16 (2), 22, 23, 26, 27 (2), 28, 29, 31, 42 (a, b), 44

IMAGNO/Peter Korrak: 103

IMAGNO/Barbara Pflaum: 47

IMAGNO/Lois Lammerhuber: 84

IMAGNO/ÖNB/Harry Weber: 46, 48, 49

IMAGNO/Schloss Schönbrunn Kultur- u. Betriebsges. m. H.: 36 (section), 40, 41

IMAGNO/Ullstein: 53, 67, 71

PRIVAT: 10, 11, 12, 69 (2)

SPANISCHE HOFREITSCHULE: 37, 108

SPANISCHE HOFREITSCHULE/René van Bakel: 81, 82, 88, 89, 96 b, 97, 105 b

SPANISCHE HOFREITSCHULE/Gabriele Boisselle: Umschlag Rückseite, 50, 51, 54/55, 56, 57, 60, 61, 62, 63 (2)

SPANISCHE HOFREITSCHULE/Peter Burgstaller: 52, 58 a, 59, 64

SPANISCHE HOFREITSCHULE/Herbert Graf: 20 (3), 21 (3), 24, 32/33, 35(2), 72 (3), 73, 74 (2), 83, 86, 87 (2), 91 a, 92, 93, 94, 96 a, 98 a, 99, 100, 109

SPANISCHE HOFREITSCHULE/Paul Harris: 6

SPANISCHE HOFREITSCHULE/Ines Hubinger: 58 b

SPANISCHE HOFREITSCHULE/Peter Rigaud: 3, 30, 34, 70, 101, 104, 105 a

SPANISCHE HOFREITSCHULE/Michael Rzepa: 66, 76, 77 (2), 78, 79, 90, 102, 106/107

SPANISCHE HOFREITSCHULE/Kunsthistorisches Museum, Wien: 17 (2), 19, 39, 43

SPANISCHE HOFREITSCHULE/United States Information Service: 45

SPANISCHE HOFREITSCHULE–BUNDESGESTÜT PIBER/Jan J. A. Hohmann: 65

The numbers denote the number of pages, the numbers in brackets denote the number of photographs.

Bibliographic information published by the Deutsche Nationalbibliothek
The Deutsche Nationalbibliothek lists this publication in the
Deutsche Nationalbibliografie; detailed bibliographic data
are available in the Internet at http://dnb.d-nb.de

1ˢᵗ edition

Cover design: Christian Brandstätter
Layout: Barbara Sternthal
Reproduction of the images: Pixelstorm, Vienna
Printing and binding in the EU

ISBN 978-3-85033-424-2

Christian Brandstätter Verlagsgesellschaft m.b.H. & Co. KG
A-1080 Vienna, Wickenburggasse 26
Telephone (+43-1) 512 15 43-0
Fax (+43-1) 512 15 43-231
E-Mail: info@cbv.at
www.cbv.at